Praise for Jane Yolen

"*Things to Say to a Dead Man* is a stunning book. What Jane Yolen offers the reader is nothing but the truth: this is what grief looks like, sounds like, smells, like, feels like. Only one who has loved so deeply can mourn this profoundly. Finely crafted and full of gorgeous imagery, every single word is an arrow that pierces the heart."

> — *Lesléa Newman, Poet Laureate of Northampton, MA 2008-2010, author of* Nobody's Mother

"If a life is measured by what is left behind, then these raw, honest and accomplished poems are a defining tribute to a husband treasured far beyond words. These are poems that come from a fathomless hole in the heart, and they tell not only of unimaginable sorrow, but of a long and remarkable marriage, built on the pleasures of love, on felicity to family, on laughter—and on birdsong. Jane Yolen is right when she says that 'no one can tell a griever how to grieve,' but this book will be welcome and wise company to those who suffer the loss of someone deeply cherished."

> — *Patricia Lee Lewis, author of* High Lonesome

Poetry Books by Jane Yolen

Among Angels
(with Nancy Willard; Harcourt, 1995)

The Radiation Sonnets: For My Love in Sickness and in Health
(Algonquin, 2003)

Things to Say to a Dead Man

Poems at the End of a Marriage and After

Jane Yolen

Holy Cow! Press :: Duluth, Minnesota :: 2011

First printing, 2011

ISBN 978-09833254-0-6

10 9 8 7 6 5 4 3 2 1

Library of Congress Cataloging-in-Publication Data

Yolen, Jane.
    Things to say to a dead man : poems at the end of a marriage and after / by Jane Yolen.
    p. cm.
    ISBN 978-0-9833254-0-6 (alk. paper)
    I. Title.
    PS3575.O43T43 2011
    811'.54—dc22 2011011302

This project is supported in part by grant awards from the Ben and Jeanne Overman Charitable Trust, the Elmer L. and Eleanor J. Andersen Foundation, the Cy and Paula DeCosse Fund of the Minneapolis Foundation, and by gifts from individual donors.

Holy Cow! Press books are distributed to the trade by Consortium Book Sales & Distribution, c/o Perseus Distribution, 1094 Flex Drive, Jackson, TN 38301.

For inquiries, please write to: Holy Cow! Press, Post Office Box 3170, Mount Royal Station, Duluth, MN 55803. www.holycowpress.org

To the Memory of David W. Stemple and his gallant five-year battle with cancer.

With special thanks to my three children and their spouses who helped me through the last plus five years. To Corinne Demas, Zane Kotker, and Lesléa Newman who heard a number of these poems and pushed for revisions, even past the pain. To Bud Webster for his enthusiasm. And to Elizabeth Harding who never gives up.

Contents

IV. And After

Acknowledgments 58

About the Author 59

Preface:

Widow First and All Else a Far Second

These poems come from the months before my husband died and the hard five years after. No one can tell a griever how to grieve. Some do it with elegance—viz Jacqueline Kennedy—and some without—like one of my aunts who used to try and fling herself into whatever open grave was at hand, sobbing loudly.

Somehow it doesn't seem to matter if what is being grieved is a good marriage, a good death, or a lousy marriage and/or a stunningly hideous death. Grief arrives in many guises and carries with it many surprises.

In the months after my husband of 44 years died (we were 46 years together), two of my cousins lost their husbands, several of my elderly aunts passed away, five friends ranging in age from 34 to 96 went, and then my favorite cousin died in a matter of days of a cancer no one had diagnosed till it was vastly too late. It was an awful couple of years.

But of course for me, the worst was my gallant, brilliant, gonzo husband leaving after a five year battle (three years in remission) with an adenocarcinoma that manifested as a massive tumor in his skull base. He left three wonderful children devastated by his death and their spouses and children, three brothers and their families, my brother and his wife and children, and of course my husband's friends, colleagues at the University of Massachusetts, the young professors and professional staff and students he'd mentored, and birders all over the world who'd been touched by his wisdom and humor.

The process of grieving is neither linear nor predictable. Each grief runs its own course. In many ways, I am still in mine.

— Jane Yolen

I
The Dying

Things to Say to a Dying Man

There, there.
It's all right.
Eat a little more, please.
Did you hear that crow?
Hush.
Hush.
I'll get that for you.
Eat a little more.
The sky is like a silver ingot
breaking into pieces of eight.
There, there.
Everything's all right.
The Carolina wren is singing our song,
a loud throaty burble,
like seltzer bubbles up the nose.
There, there.
Hush.
Hush.
It's all right.
The woodpeckers have cut a strip
off the walnut tree
big as a plowed field.
Do you think it's going to snow?
There, there.
It's all right.
Hush.
Hush.
We have robins in the yard,
red breasts puffed out,
striding like proud farmers
across the greening grass.
There, there.
It's all right.
Eat a little more, please.
I love you.

Parts of Speech

This is my husband lying in the bed.
This was my husband lying in the bed.
I am having trouble
with even the simplest of verbs.
By *was* do I mean he is dead
even though I can see a shallow bird breath
beating beneath the cage of his chest bones?
Or am I remembering
a taller man, straight-backed,
who drew his oxygen right from the air?

This is my husband lying in the bed.
Lying is an interesting word,
Meaning prone
or prone to untruths
like a beautiful woman
who lies because she can,
not because she has to.
Besides, he may be laying down not lying,
a part of speech I have never gotten right,
no matter how many poems I have written.

This is my husband lying in the bed.
Why do we say *in*,
as if he is stuffed inside the mattress,
a feather of a man,
"a cloud in trousers," as he often quoted,
as we spooned together on the squeaky brass bed,
which is how I became
acquainted with Mayakovsky.
And now my old cloud,
you are so thin and wispy,
it hurts to settle down beside you.

This is my husband lying in the bed.
How proprietal that *my* looks,
out of place with the rest of the sentence,
as if forty-six years beside him
gives me a kind of ownership.
One cannot own this man
any more than one can own a wild bird
that places its allegiance
to wind and sky and sometimes,
sometimes,
to a single mate.

Hospital Bed

At night, trying to sleep
on the futon by his side,
I listen as my husband's fingers
play with the buttons
on his hospital bed.
I have grown to hate the bloody thing,
which creaks at all hours
like a dotty cuckoo clock,
the feet rising, lowering,
the head moving up and down.
Then, Jesus!
as if it is the main attraction
at a Victorian séance,
the whole bed rises up,
its sheet and floral coverlet
flowing outward like angel wings.
It is the ghost at the banquet,
Mesmer's inheritance,
David Copperfield's best trick.
I lie awake until dawn
contemplating spiritualism,
that counter to the dangerous
currents of science
which flow so deadly in his veins.
I could kill my husband now
in the middle of the night,
if I weren't so intent
on keeping him alive.

Smells

The dying man does not smell
like the living man,
he smells of old pee and unwashed teeth,
of sugar drinks and protein shakes the color of prunes.
He smells of sweet decay.

When my mother died,
my youngest child was nine days old,
smelling of baby lotion and talc.
I could breathe him in all day.
I couldn't remember my mother's smell.
Going into her closet, I closed the door.
Chanel No. 5 still lingered
on the shoulders of her camel's hair coat,
and Ban roll-on had sunk under
the arms of her jackets.
For a moment she was alive.

All I have here are my husband's shirts
covered with milky spills,
and his pajama bottoms smelling of pee.
I want that heathery, yellow soap man back,
the one who I spent most of my life
sniffing like a dog in heat.

Oxygen

I wish I understood chemistry,
had listened better in class,
oh, fifty years ago,
in that odd, ugly high school lab,
so that oxygen isn't such a mystery.
I get the plastic connectors,
the big silver tank humped like a dowager,
the little plastic nipples in my husband's nose.
The constant soft hiss
of gas disappearing up his nostrils
has the reassurance of a lullaby.

But why a colorless, odorless, tasteless gas
can change his expression
from slack to comprehending—
that is a mystery so profound,
I doubt even Priestly could explain it.
The twelve good oarsmen of 1621,
who rowed under the Thames
at a depth of fifteen feet
from Westminster to Greenwich,
were kept alive in their barbaric submarine
by their trust in their leader,
and in part by oxygen.
A miracle by some standards, science by others.

Chemistry I do not understand, but metaphor I do.
My husband is like those rowers,
swimming up from the depth of his cancers,
kept alive in part by oxygen,
and in part by my great love.

Two Singers Sing Away the Pain: A Triolet

Two singers sing away the pain,
One singing lieder, one singing folk.
Outside the world is washed with rain
As two singers sing away the pain
Of the cancer settled beneath his brain,
God's idea of a cosmic joke.
But two singers sing away the pain,
One singing lieder and one singing folk.

(*With thanks to Matthew Roehrig and Lui Collins, the two singers*)

The Good Wife

The good wife cleans her husband's bum,
Wipes the spills from his beard,
Turns the oxygen to 2.5,
Rubs his feet with warm oil,
Cuts his toenails and fingernails,
Does not dream of *After*
When her bed will be lonely,
Her children off to their own lives,
And she is thought to be—
Ought to be—
Sexless and alone.

The good wife cleans the pee pot,
The pink plastic vomitorium,
Puts good soup in the blender,
Makes protein shakes twice a day,
Counts out the pills and the eye drop meds,
Makes sure there is enough prune juice,
And Tucks pads, and lotions.
She does not schedule too many friends for visits,
Or write an obit early
Or plan a memorial service before it is time,
In case that's a curse.

The good wife needs no manuals from Hospice,
No hand holding, no therapists,
No friends with chicken soup,
No one to say "You're brave,"
No one to do the laundry,
Get the groceries, clean the kitchen,
Change the bed linens and the cat litter.

No, the good wife does it all alone,
Then lies down on the pyre
Next to her dearly beloved
And goes up with him in a pure blaze to heaven.

Sitting Down to Eat

How many times did we sit down to eat
And you refused the offering?
One time, ten times, a hundred times,
Your mouth sore, your stomach drawn in on itself,
The cancer like some tin-hat dictator
Forbidding you your life. How many times?

How many times did I make soup, straining it
In the blender: tomato, apple, butternut squash,
Sweetening it to tempt you, decorating the dish.
There was nothing I would not try,
Even buying a second blender to be ready
Should you want to eat again. How many times?

Each spoonful a victory, I cozened you
As if you were a reluctant child, begging,
Singing, telling you tales, the old choo-choo,
Spoon chugging into your mouth.
I did not go quite that far, but would have,
Had I thought it would work, many times.

And on the last day, though we didn't know it
Till after, you ate an extra spoonful, winked
At your son. We didn't say a word, not one,
So astonished, we took it for a sign
You were on the mend, relaxed our guard,
And you slipped away. No more time.

Coma

Never so still, not even in the field,
The birds haranguing you with song
And you whispering into the recorder
Their names, the dates of their singing.
Never so quiet, even in our bed,
Where we laughed between embraces,
Or silently read our books, our notes,
Or worked crosswords too hard for just one of us.
Never so still, not even at the birth
Of your daughter, your sons,
Counting the smallness of their toes,
The fine hairs on heads the size of your hands.
Never so still as this before, though I know
That you will be stiller yet,
While my body will shake with years of weeping
Until it is my time to be so still.

II
The Dead Man

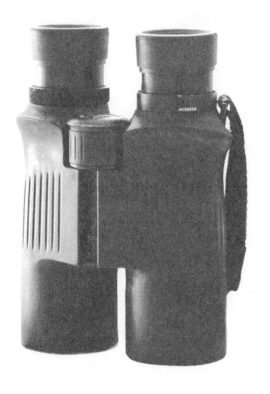

After He Died

Did he see his daughter with her daughter
frantically driving home
from their New York City holiday,
her car maneuvering potholes
more surely than she maneuvered
the sudden hole in her heart?
Did he see her fighting the tears,
her nine-year old daughter's fear
of returning to the house of death?
Did he know they would walk in
find themselves relieved
that his body was already gone?
Did he sigh like a whisper of wind,
or laugh with the freedom of letting go
of that thinned-out old body,
with the Auschwitz legs and protruding ribs,
the blinded eyes, the ears that could no longer hear
the difference between crow and not-crow?
Did he shake his head, finding himself
out of body, in the ether, perilously close
to some great being called God?
Or did he just, as he always supposed,
simply evaporate, becoming earth and sky,
ember and ash and, at the last, birdsong.

Sorry for Your Loss

I have not misplaced him—
like the wedding ring
he left behind at a ski lodge
six months after we married.
I have only set him aside
in a small grave
under a tree where robins sing.
They are thrushes, you know,
and their songs pierce,
especially at six in the morning
in the early spring.

I did not lose him,
except the smell of him,
already cleansed by chemicals,
flensed in the fire,
that reduced him to an essence
that can be blown into glass.
But the pillow that cradled
that dear head at the end
still carries his scent
which has the power to reduce me,
sunder me, render me,
into globules of fat tears.

I did not leave him behind,
but let him go ahead—
the pathfinder, map reader,
who knew the compass points—
finding a shortcut
which always meandered,
leading us inexorably
into brilliant discoveries
like the last manned Scottish lighthouse
on the very last manned day.

I will follow, my love,
maybe not soon,
but soon enough
to wherever you have gone,
not waiting for me,
but preparing the way,
for you will have already
identified the birds
and learned their songs,
in your new world,
ready to teach me
all the things I have to know.

Single Malt

Across the field we went,
whiskey in hand
to pour it on your grave,
a libation to you
and the gods you did not believe in.
Bluebirds and robins sang overhead,
and we were careful to spill the drinks
right on your grave
lest you scold us for wasting it.
Wee David carried a ball
bigger than his head.
Alison and Maddison had flowers
plucked from the forty-seven bouquets
friends and relatives sent.
We all hauled memories
along the caked earth,
memories of you before the cancer,
and after when you were so much smaller.
Still, I cannot believe you fit
into that tiny grave,
when what I remember is so large
it cracks me open every morning,
splitting me like a well-placed wedge.

Coming into Town

Coming into town, the dogwood buds like popcorn,
White and perfect, I think of you,
Hand in the overflowing bucket
At the movies, threatening not to share.

Coming into town, the magnolias melting flowers,
Petals drifting down, I think of you,
Standing beneath the trees, laughing,
At something you said yourself.

Coming into town, birdsong bursting,
Bragging about the air, the land, the ladies,
I think of you, standing on a mountaintop,
Holding up a microphone
Recording ring ouzels in the Highlands.

Coming into town, the flowers
On either side of the street straining
To open, I think of you beneath
The earth, no longer straining
To do anything at all, and that is the hardest thing,
The hardest thing, the very hardest thing
To remember as I come into town.

Rain

Finally, finally it has rained on your grave.
I have been waiting for that pathetic fallacy
to make complete what my mind still does not
comprehend.

The rain was misty, moisty,
the cemetery suitably gray, wet stones and moss.
The tree limb over your grave wept.
It looked like a true death this time,
not the sunshine and soft wind and bird song
that accompanied you
before.

I sat for a long time in the car crying,
then got out, to tell you what I was feeling.
The rain curled my hair.
Speaking to you this way is so unsatisfactory.
You do not answer,
who always had an answer for
everything.

Five Breaths

How to measure a life?
Not by the time from birth,
when you must have come
squalling into the light.
But by the quiet hush
after you were gone.

Five breaths as I held your hand.
Five breaths shuddering,
as if the three-storied house
and all that is stuffed in it
was shaken by the wind
of your dying.

Five breaths, and all that time
I was alive when you were alive.
In the hush after,
though I kept on breathing,
I could not call that life.

Now all the days, months,
daft moments, the birdsong,
naming of trees,
our grandson's small fist in your face,
the walks on Scottish Munroes,
count as nothing.

Five breaths.
In the end
that was all I had of you
before you took them away
and left me with only my own.

How Am I Doing, Really?

You do not want me to answer that,
for it would mean peeling back my skin
splitting open my chest bones,
revealing a heart that still beats
though it is half the size it once was.
It would mean sawing off the top of my skull
and shaking out pieces of my brain
which hardly functions right, left
are memories, the latest ones first,
like daguerreotypes nestled in a velvet lining,
you dead on the bed, your head to one side,
mouth open, an image that is with me always.

How am I doing, really? Really well
on the outside, so that everyone seeing me
murmurs, "So brave, so astonishing,"
while inside I am climbing onto that last bed,
spooning my body around yours,
and dying even more slowly than you did.

Things to Say to a Grieving Woman

There, there.
It's all right.
Eat a little more, please.
Was that a crow?
Hush.
Hush.
I'll get that for you.
Eat a little more.
How about those Red Sox?
Did you read Atwood's latest?
There, there.
Everything's all right.
I seem to be having trouble
finding the paper napkins,
should we use cloth this time?
There, there.
Hush.
Hush.
It's all right.
I built you a bluebird house.
Is there somewhere
you want it?
Do you think it's going to snow?
There, there.
It's all right.
Hush.
Hush.
Maybe you could come for dinner
Next Sunday,
Monday,
Tuesday
Friday.
There, there.
It's all right.

Eat a little more,
please.
We love you.

III
First Year

Two Months Later

My friends expect me to be over
the worst of the grief;
that writing, dinners, the occasional lunch,
meetings, a movie or two,
work on our daughter's house,
two conferences in states far away
will scab over the deep cut
below my breastbone
where your death removed my heart.

The heart, like a phantom limb,
still hurts, throbs, aches, agonizes
over familiar things. Your shirts
hanging in the closet,
the dozen or so hats you loved,
shoes two sizes big for me,
three sizes too small for our sons.
I cannot yet bear to give them away
to the homeless, the shelters,
the needy, when my need
for you is still so great.

Do not help me to forget.
Help me to remember.

Second Time Around

Here, in our second house,
I must do everything again.
Your clothes, still smelling of you,
must be washed, sorted, given away.
Notes in your handwriting
carry your thoughts into the future,
alas, not terribly deep
but more poignant for that:
a grocery list, how to stand at golf,
where to stay in the Pyrenees,
the Latin names of certain birds.
It is as if you died a second time
and I must bury you again
out in the garden,
the peonies weeping you down.
I do not begrudge you more tears.
I remember, instead, the joy we had,
here in this second house,
stone built, with its back lawn
so green beneath the Scottish skies,
it feels as if your ashes are scattered
on the sea, not the ground.

Sunday Trip to London

Grey funnel of rain on the horizon,
a settlement of sheep cropping the grass,
the single fishing boat rocking in soft waves,
white button flowers tangling in the wind,
rose bay willow herb surprising the borders.
All this I observe while the train rolls along,
as I try to escape my ongoing grief
by riding down to London.
Six hours south is not nearly enough,
for grief rides with me in First Class,
drinking tea, reading the papers, even a dip
into Jane Austen. Such a proper companion,
never once speaking out of turn.
I should have stayed at home, where tears
are no embarrassment and conductors
do not inquire about one's health.
Home, where you are safely stowed
underground in the garden,
and I can visit you every hour
without the need of a ticket or an unfamiliar bed.

I Have Not Forgotten

I have not forgotten
but I do not think of your death
every day. Though sometimes
the memories overwhelm me
and I pull the car over
to weep by the roadside.
In this land of clouds and rain,
no one notices a wet face.
If I am to live,
then I have to go on
down all the winding roads,
stopping only briefly,
as if to let faster cars by.
The other drivers will not know
the stop is occasioned by tears
which, for the small moment,
have made driving impossible,
tears that are indistinguishable
from the Highland rains.

First Fall

This is my first fall without,
The leaves redder than I remember.
Not the color of blood, which dries dark
But something more vibrant
In its long dying.

This is my first fall without,
The mornings so cold, I wear
One of your old sweaters over my nightgown
And turn up the heat till the house
Breaks out in a sweat.

This is my first fall without,
The hardy horse chestnuts—
Conkers you called them—
Banging down on the roof slates
All night long, pocking the car.

This is my first fall without,
The geese in their dyslexic vees
That sometimes read like an *L* or *M*,
Head to where Connecticut and Massachusetts
Huddle together for warmth.

This is my first fall without.
You have gone before me into winter,
Into spring, into summer, somehow
A consummate time traveler
I can never catch up to,
Always a season ahead.

First Frost

1.

How crisp the leaves underfoot,
This first real frost,
Crimping the edges of maple,
Discoloring the chestnut.
The hem of my heart wears the same frost
As I go into my first winter without you.
I hope you are not cold in all the places
I have sown your ashes,
Hoping for resurrection in the spring.

2.

This is a year of farewells.
Every month carries old memories.
This week a year ago, the battle lines
Had been clearly drawn.
You were winning, but at a horrid cost.
Would I have had you pay
Knowing then what I know now?

3.

Another year another frost,
I imagine the time,
How hard and cold my heart will be,
Leaf mold beneath the rime.

Gone to Ground

Even the chickadees
in their every-day black tams,
remind me of you, who taught me to see
the extraordinary in such ordinary natures.
How ring ouzels sing with local dialects,
green herons make tools for fishing,
and spring robins by the thousands
roost in our February plantations of fir.
Who will tell me these things,
show me out the corner of the eye,
the stoop of hawk, the silence of the owl,
now that you have gone to ground
like some old rogue on the run?

Christmas Bird Count Night: 2006

This was the time you would get out of bed,
dress in double layers, thick socks,
stick granola bars in your pockets,
check the owl map, make the milky sweet tea,
hot water in the thermos first
to warm it.

This was the time I would mumble
"Should I get up?" and throw back the covers,
counting on you to tell me to sleep in,
take advantage of the fresh warmth,
from your side of the queen-size bed,
closest to the door.

This was the time I would be grateful for sleep,
for being the one staying home with the kids,
making breakfast for the bird count folk,
out all night in the cold, the snow, the ice, the dark,
while I nestled in our snuggle of blankets,
oblivious to owls.

This was the time you should be here,
not strewn across two continents
in little clumps of cold ash and scorched bone
while the owls, like faithless lovers,
answer any old birder who calls them out
on bird count night.

Wading Back

From my bedroom window,
our daughter's house is dark,
no lights to indicate she's up
writing, bathing, eating second-day salad.
I lie in my widow's bed trying to guess,
as if that makes me a partner in her life.
It's a kind of voyeurism, without longing.
Except—if I could—I'd slip back forty years,
before her house was even considered,
There you are, marking the path ahead,
and me behind, a child in my arms,
wading through the thigh-high grass,
which like life needs taming,
until we grow old wishing for the wildness,
the overgrowth, the feral to grow back again.

Chinese Proverb Sent by A Worried Friend

"If I keep a green bough in my heart, the singing bird will come."

Hell, if it works, I will rototill the ventricle
and dig down to the aorta,
plant the largest damned baobab I can find,
set strobe lights on the tree's trunk,
put out feeding stations along each green bough.
That bird can be as insistent a singer
as the Carolina wren on my back deck,
the one I've dubbed Elvis
and sometimes Billy Ray Cyrus,
because he hollers and struts
every morning just before breakfast,
long as he's sure I'm listening,
me and my hunk o', hunk o' achy breaky heart.

A Matter of Fact

Your grandson looks up, says, "Papa is dead,"
then goes on playing with his cars,
as if "dead" is simply a new place you live,
not here, but somewhere out of sight.
I suppose he has the right of it,
but it does not solve the heart
or salve the heart or safe the heart.
I wish I could be four again,
and know you are dead without the pain of it,
a matter of fact like stars stick in the sky
snow is white, mud icky, ice cream cold,
and grandfathers die.
Never mind why.

You in the House: A Holiday Lament

My eardrums have grown thin
trying to hear your voice one more time.
Laughter and bright lights—
menorah, tree it does not matter—
all hurt my ears, my eyes,
the imprint of you lying dead
still ragged on the inside of my lids.
The smells of fir tree and incense and candles
cannot erase the odor of your head on the pillow,
or the robe I have refused to wash.
But what I miss most is your touch,
the curve of your back against my belly at night,
your hand in mine as we walk in the deep woods,
our thighs next to one another's on a plane
your lips in my hair, on my neck, my breasts.
There is no more sense of you in the house,
only photos, static, single-planed,
more still than you were in life.
I try to dream of you, your breath, your laugh,
your humbugging the holiday,
but it's forced, not real,
not real enough, not enough.

Taking Your Clothes to the Salvation Army

Okay, not all of them, but the washed socks,
the clean white handkerchiefs and boxer shorts
that your sons don't want; not the Orvis shirts
or the hand-made scarves, or the hats
with sweat bands that still smell of you.
Three bags of stuff, as if the detritus
of a well-lived life is summed up at the Sally
where a man too roughly accepts your hand-me-downs.

Okay, so strangers will be grateful for this,
will wear the socks to keep their feet warm,
blow their noses in your handkerchiefs,
pull up the shorts, tuck in the size large shirts,
(too small for our boys, too big for our daughter)
and bits of you will be out there,
engaging in a life you no longer have.

I should be happy for that bit of recycling,
but I would be happier still
warming you with my naked body in our bed
no hats, scarves, shirts, boxers, socks.

The Bull

In my dream last night you were a bull,
running through the woods, shaking your head,
your horns slashing the lowest limbs.
There was power in your running,
your black hooves pounding the ground.
I'd forgotten how powerful you were once,
recalling only the last terrible days,
when you had to lean on me to get to the chair,
the kitchen table, the toilet, the shower,
an old bull then, head down, shaking,
ready for the knacker.

Journey

This long trip away from you,
from the corporeal to the memory,
not a highway but a brutal track,
potholed and overgrown with weeds,
takes a greater toll than I imagined.
I am footsore from the journey.
Road signs have been removed.
Maps are filled with erasures.
Books by similar travelers
do not help me on my way.
Every road is different;
every road the same.
I do not know where I am going
or what I will do when I get there.
I know only that to put one foot
in front of the other, moves me on,
away from you to a place,
where I do not want to be.

David Moments

A flock of turkeys parading before us,
as we make our way to the common room
being dedicated in your memory;
the mallard guarding his mate in the library atrium
at the very moment I give a speech about you;
a ring ouzel jumping up on the rock
where your ashes have just been spread;
the drunken pheasant careening down the sidewalk
whom I laughingly invite into the garden,
finding it an hour later calling
from the top of the Monkey Puzzle tree.
I am not alone in these odd sightings.
Friends over the world report them to me.
David's come calling, they say,
fully aware of the double meaning,
you old bird song specialist,
knowing you would laugh loudest at the joke.

Anniversary of Your Death

We sat in the living room
amid candles, flowers, photographs,
reading letters about your life,
all we have left of you.
You were never so flat, so one-sided,
able to fit single-spaced on a white page.
You were the one who burst into a room,
your mind cartwheeling over every listener.
You shaped and reshaped our interests,
told us multilingual jokes,
your intelligence fierce enough
to shake the foundations of our house.
Yet you could be so silent,
birds sang entire repertoires
into your parabolic ear.

What we captured on that single page,
while we sat surrounded
by flower smells and flickering candles,
were but captions, footnotes, citations,
though only echoes—like the tapes of your bird songs,
short phrases of melody, soaring always upward—
remain.

IV
And After

The Garden in April

Some small green shoots have already
broken out into daffodil grins.
Bunched roots of peonies
point green fingers toward the sky.
Dogwood and magnolia have burst
blossoms at the seams.
As always iris and lilies spread
like Attila and his hordes
across borders, counties, countries.

It is spring. Everything in nature returns.
Everything.
So why are you not here,
rising up from my garden
as you used to rise up from our bed?
From the brass double bed where our children
slept with us, or the new wooden bed
queen size, big enough for two complicated sleepers
after the children had gone out on their own.
Or the hospital bed, single and sterile,
where you died in the middle of a March thaw.

April has returned to me everything,
everything but what means the most,
for I can dig deep in the garden,
down below the root system
and still not find you.

The Stone

I saw your stone today
lying flat on the back of a truck.
Horrible how a man's whole life
is summed up in several short lines
chiseled in the granite:
name, birth, death.
Words like "teacher" and "father" define
the accomplished years.
It is shorthand, caption, text message, twitter,
biography in the small,
when you were so large
that only I could read entirely
between the lines.

Neglect

As I could not neglect you in life,
I'll not neglect you in death,
nor leave your gravestone
sulking in a hedge.
In fact your stone stands tall
beneath a weeping tree,
and we have plans—
we always have plans—
to plant perennials at its foot,
if time and sun and rain
and my aching knees allow.
I expect our daughter
will do the planting,
and I the praying.
It is a partnership
that works well for us
in death as in life.

Grief Is Not

Grief is not getting easier,
But becoming more ordinary,
As if I've always carried this stone in my breast,
Calling it a heart.

Grief is not going away,
Just not arriving in tsunami force.
Rather it's a steady high tide,
Which makes me wonder about the rocks below.

Grief is not a one-time thing,
Not several days, weeks, months,
But is a visitor who has moved in for good,
And occasionally helps out around the house.

Grief is not unwelcome here,
For it reminds me of how much I have lost,
And how blessed I was
To have so much to lose.

Goodbye Billy Goat Gruff

How many bridges had we traveled
always looking ahead,
constantly moving, never still.
You would have stayed awhile more
If you could, but there was that final bridge,
That toll, that green—and you were gone.

Cemetery in the Snow

The town had not plowed the road
and so I sat shivering in the car
while a solitary crow crossed
over your stone marker, cawing.
If I had wings I could have visited,
told you about your twin granddaughters,
how they finish one another's sentences.
Gossip like story keeps us alive
even you, in your underground chamber.
So the crow's raucous message
was the only voice you heard,
and what kind of tidings was that?
I will try again in a few weeks
to bring you the family news,
when spring's excavation
uncovers the path to your eternity.
I hope you will take the time to listen.

Resignation

I am resigned,
Though I said I was not at your funeral.
My heart is taking a by-pass
On the living road.
The future does not concern me.
I like the certainty of what once was.
Now I ride in airplanes unafraid.
I write but do not contemplate publication.
I no longer plan my daughter's remarriage,
My sons' job prospects,
My grandchildren's lives.
I wish I had known resignation earlier.
It is a good neighbor,
And a comforting friend.

Third Yahrzeit

I will light a candle for you today,
this third anniversary of your death.
I will read your single love poem to me aloud.
I will remember things you said,
though not your voice,
somehow never your voice
which must have been burned away
in the crematorium.
Three years is a long time,
a short time,
a rubber band time
stretching and contracting
according to the weather, the season,
whether my back hurts or my rebuilt knee,
politics and what Faux News reports,
how well the writing goes or doesn't,
birdsong, chocolate, or the time of day.
What a journey of three years this has been.
I move on, go past, but carry a long train behind
Occasionally, rounding a serious bend,
I spot the caboose
and see you waving, like an addled conductor,
still collecting tickets
though the passengers have all left.,
I wave back and then, another bend,
And you are gone again.

This Is the Morning After His Death: A Triolet

This is the morning after his death
Though three years in the past.
I watched him take his final breath,
But this is the morning after his death.
There is no height, nor underneath,
There is no slow, there is no fast,
Only this morning after his death,
Though three years in the past.

Things to Say to a Widow

You're looking good.
Feeling well?
Short answer, not long.
Must get together.
Have you seen the latest Mirren film?
Read a book?
You're looking fine.
Have you lost weight?
How are those grandkids?
Must get together.
Written much?
Been on a trip?
Like the spring?
Must get together.
You're looking good.
Feeling fine?
Lost some weight?
New haircut?
Must
get
together
soon.

Fifth Year Anniversary

Feels like yesterday.
Feels like a door closing.
Feels like a door opening.
I lit three golden candles.
Placed two containers
of small, furled rosebuds
on either side of the table,
the blown glass globe
with some of his ashes
between the buds.
Is this the end of the poetry
of our lives together?
Sometimes I feel as if
I'm in the heart's desert,
sand slowing my footsteps.
Lizards scuttle away from me.
A solitary buzzard flies overhead.
I am weary but not worried.
The world stills turns
and so do I.
Crossing the desert has its own beauty.

Acknowledgments:

"Smells," *Doorways Magazine* (#7, October 2008)

"Parts of Speech," Smith College Poetry Center website (2008)

"After He Died," *Doorways Magazine* (#5, March 2008)

"Every Day," *Doorways Magazine* (#7, October 2008)

"Five Breaths," *Helix Magazine* (2008)

"How Am I Doing, Really?" *Doorways Magazine* (#6, June 2008)

"Two Months Later," *Living with Grief: Before and After the Death*, Hospice Foundation (2007)

"First Fall," *Telling the True* (2006)

"Chinese Proverb Sent By A Worried Friend," *Helix Magazine* (2007/8)

"The Bull," *Helix Magazine* (2007)

"Journey," *Doorways Magazine* (#7, October 2008)

"Goodbye Billy Goat Gruff," *Asimov's Magazine* (2008)

"This Is the Morning After His Death: A Triolet," *Miss Rumphius Effect* (2009)

"Third Yahrzeit," *Telling the True* (2009)

About the Author

Jane Yolen, often called "the Hans Christian Andersen of America," is the author of over 300 books, including *Owl Moon, The Devil's Arithmetic,* and *How Do Dinosaurs Say Goodnight.* The books range from rhymed picture books and baby board books, through middle grade fiction, poetry collections, nonfiction, and up to novels and story collections for young adults and adults. Her adult poetry has been published in literary journals, anthologies, and magazines.

Dr. Yolen's books and stories have won an assortment of awards—two Nebulas, a World Fantasy Award, a Caldecott, the Golden Kite Award, three Mythopoetic awards, two Christopher Medals, a nomination for the National Book Award, and the Jewish Book Award, among others. She is also the winner (for body of work) of the Kerlan Award, the 2012 de Grummond Medal, the World Fantasy Association Lifetime Achievement Award, and the Catholic Library's Regina Medal. Six colleges and universities have given her honorary doctorates. If you need to know more about her, visit her website at: www.janeyolen.com